SCHOLASTIC

Follow-the-Directions
All About Me

Kama Einhorn

NEW YORK • TORONTO • LONDON • AUCKLAND • SYDNEY
MEXICO CITY • NEW DELHI • HONG KONG • BUENOS AIRES

Teaching *Resources*

Cover design: Maria Lilja
Interior design: Kathy Massaro
Illustrations: Rusty Fletcher

ISBN: 978-0-545-32959-0

Text © 2012 by Kama Einhorn
Illustrations © 2012 by Scholastic Inc.

Published by Scholastic Inc.

Contents

Here I Am!

My Friends & Family

Learn & Play

Special Times & Holidays

Favorite Foods

Amazing Animals

Wishes & Dreams

About This Book

In this book, you'll find 40 pages that combine two very different—but equally important—early elementary themes: following directions and "all about me."

As you know, following directions is crucial to school success. For a variety of reasons, many children need extra practice following multiple-step directions, both written and spoken. This book provides them with 40 hands-on opportunities to do just that.

Following directions, of course, is a foundational skill not just in school, but also in life. Virtually every task requires some sort of direction-following, even when the result is open ended. It's an important part of functioning within a group. Individually, it's important to tune into written and spoken directions because they so often set the stage for success. (You can't bake without a recipe unless you've made that recipe many times!) In the classroom, directions also provide a needed structure, an organized approach for an environment that may become chaotic without them.

Besides providing practice in following directions, each of these 40 pages is highly personal and engaging! "All about me" is a common social studies theme for a great developmental reason: kids start to understand the world first by understanding and expressing themselves. It is only then that they develop empathy and learn that they are similar to (and different from) others in ways big and small. From there, they can understand the way communities function, and later, the way the world works.

By completing these pages, kids will be able to communicate a lot of information about themselves in a structured format, without having to write more than they are able. They'll share and describe their likes and dislikes, their very favorite things, their family and friends, their fantasies and dreams, and more.

By combining the two key themes of following directions and "all about me," you'll help kids function better in the classroom—while explaining to themselves and others who they are. These reproducible pages are quick and easy ways to do that. Enjoy watching your students' procedural skills grow along with their self-awareness!

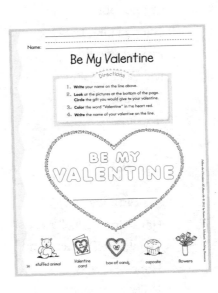

What's Inside

Each of the 40 activity pages is a stand-alone activity with its own topic and directions. The pages can be used in any order. However, all of the pages are the same in several ways:

❋ The directions are always at the top of the page and always in the same numbered format.

❋ There are always four steps. This is a common number of steps that children need to follow, and gives you the opportunity to use procedural words, such as *first, next, then,* and *last* when discussing these directions.

❋ The activity pages can be used for independent, small-group, or whole-group work, as well as in centers and for homework.

Directions all include the following:

❋ Key action words (in boldface to signal their importance to students) are the words most commonly used in directions: *cut, write, put, color, glue, draw, circle, underline, trace, put an X on, check, think, decide,* and so on.

❋ Positional words such as *above, below, in, next to, on, under, underneath.*

Together, the 40 pages are an "autobiography" of sorts. The pages are even arranged in seven "chapters" in each child's story: Here I Am!, My Friends & Family, Learn & Play, Special Times & Holidays, Favorite Foods, Amazing Animals, and Wishes & Dreams.

Introducing the Activities

Before you begin using the activities in this book, explain to children that these pages, like journals, are places for them to record their feelings, likes and dislikes, and experiences. Tell them that the pages will let them share all kinds of information about themselves with whoever reads them, whether it's the teacher, classmates, or family members, and that they'll be able to color and draw to personalize the pages.

Depending on children's age and level, you might want to complete one as a demonstration before asking children to work independently. For each page:

1. Copy the page for each child. You'll probably want to have all children do the same page at once so that if they are sharing them when complete, they are sharing information on the same topic. Distribute the pages.

2. Set the stage for following directions and writing and drawing by examining the page together and asking questions such as:

   * What is the title of the page?
   * Can you point to the directions box?
   * How many steps are in the directions?
   * What do the directions say to do first?
   * What do the directions say to do second?
   * What do the directions say to do next?
   * What do the directions say to do last?
   * Can you point to the number 1 (then 2, 3, and 4) in the directions?
   * Can you point to the word "circle" in the directions?
   * Can you point to the word "draw" in the directions? (and *cut, write, check, decide,* and so on).

3. Check that children are following each direction correctly and completing the steps in order.

4. Invite children to share their responses with the group or with a buddy. See Follow-Up Activities, page 7, for ideas on sharing and extending the learning.

Connections to the Common Core State Standards

The Common Core State Standards Initiative (CCSSI) has outlined learning expectations in English/Language Arts for students at different grade levels. The activities in this book align with the following standards for students in kindergarten and grade 1.

Reading Standards for Informational Text

Range of Reading and Level of Text Complexity

* K.10 Actively engage in group reading activities with purpose and understanding.
* 1.10 With prompting and support, read informational texts appropriately complex for grade 1.

Reading Standards: Foundational Skills

Print Concepts

* K.1, 1.1 Demonstrate understanding of the organization and basic features of print.

Phonics and Word Recognition

* K.3, 1.3 Know and apply grade-level phonics and word analysis skills in decoding words.

Fluency

* K.4 Read emergent-reader texts with purpose and understanding
* 1.4 Read with sufficient accuracy and fluency to support comprehension.

Language Standards

Conventions of Standard English

* K.1, 1.1 Demonstrate command of the conventions of standard English grammar and usage when writing or speaking.
* K.2, 1.2 Demonstrate command of the conventions of standard English capitalization, punctuation, and spelling when writing.

Follow-Up Activities

Make a Keepsake Book

Have children keep their completed pages in a folder. When they have completed a certain number, they can bind them together into an "autobiography." Children can make their own cover and share it with their families. Or, you might share the books with families at conference time. If you do "student of the week," that child can read his or her book to the group.

Graph It!

Use a certain page to begin a graphing exercise. Have children bring their completed pages to circle time and share their responses. Record their responses on a bar graph. For instance, after children complete Fruits and Vegetables, page 37, you might create a graph of the class's favorite fruits by asking, "How many children chose apples as their favorite fruit? How many chose bananas?" and so on.

Combine With a Lesson

Several of the pages will lend themselves to explicit teaching. For instance, It's Time!, page 25, offers a great opportunity to teach telling time, or build upon what children already know. My Quilt Design, page 23, is perfect for reviewing shapes. My Favorite Breakfast, page 32, and What's for Dinner?, page 33, are useful springboards for a discussion about healthy food choices and nutrition.

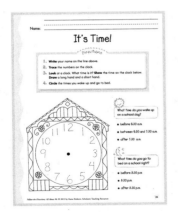

Put Them on Display

Many of the pages will make great bulletin board displays. For instance, at the beginning of the year, you might display What I Look Like, page 9, on a "Welcome to Our Class" bulletin board. At Halloween time, display children's completed Here Comes Halloween! pages, page 27.

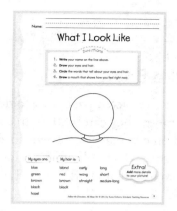

Communicate at Class Meetings

Several pages are perfect as discussion-starters at class meetings. Use Things I Like to Do, page 21, to discuss how we all have likes and dislikes, and how we are good at different things. Meet My Friend, page 15, can be a good opportunity to talk about what it means to be a friend. Even Playground Fun, page 22, can be used as a springboard into a conversation about issues that may arise on the playground.

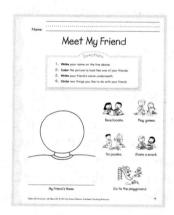

Think Critically and Classify

When all children have completed a page, help them develop critical thinking and classification skills by having them sort the pages into different categories. For instance, with My Eyes, page 11, they can group the pages according to color. As a follow-up to My Birthday, page 26, let children sort the activity sheets by birthday month and put them in chronological order.

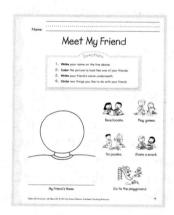

Name: _____

What I Look Like

Directions

1. **Write** your name on the line above.
2. **Draw** your eyes and hair.
3. **Circle** the words that tell about your eyes and hair.
4. **Draw** a mouth that shows how you feel right now.

My eyes are:

blue

green

brown

black

hazel

My hair is:

blond   curly   long

red   wavy   short

brown   straight   medium-long

black

Extra!
Add more details to your picture!

My Name

Directions

1. **Write** your name on the line above.

2. **Look** at the letters below.

3. **Circle** all the letters in your first name.

4. **Point** to each letter as you sing the ABC song.

A B C D E F G
H I J K L M N O
P Q R S T U V
W X Y Z

Extra!

Underline the first letter of your last name.

Name: _____

My Eyes

Directions

1. **Write** your name on the line above.
2. **Color** the eye to match your eye color.
3. **Draw** lashes on your eye.
4. **Circle** the things you see around you right now.

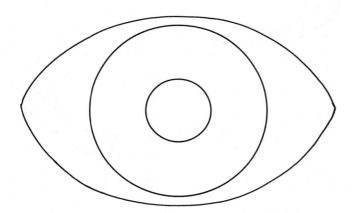

I see:

crayon

plant

children

desk

window

book

door

computer

Extra! **Draw** something else you see right now.

Follow-the-Directions: All About Me
© 2012 by Kama Einhorn,
Scholastic Teaching Resources

Name: _____

My T-Shirt

Directions

1. **Write** your name on the line above.

2. **Decide** if there will there be words on your shirt.
   Circle one: yes   no

3. **Write** or **draw** on your shirt.

4. **Color** the rest of your shirt any color you like.

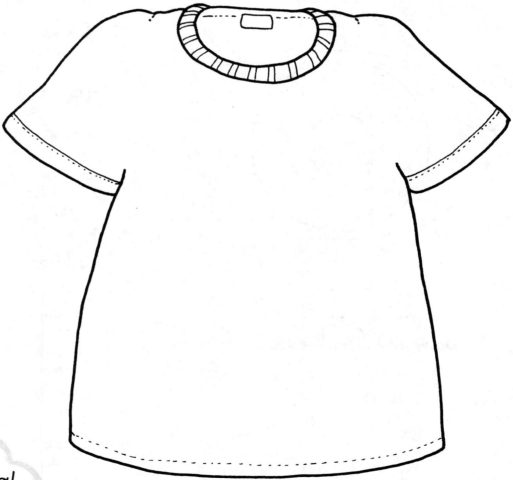

Extra!

The color of my favorite T-shirt at home is _____

Follow-the-Directions: All About Me © 2012 by Kama Einhorn, Scholastic Teaching Resources

Name: _____

Growing Up

Directions

1. **Write** your name on the line above.

2. **Draw** pictures to go with each page.

3. **Cut** the pages apart and **put** them in order.

4. **Staple** them to make a book.

I'm Growing Up!

1

Here I am when I was a baby.

2

Here I am when I was a little kid.

3

Here I am now!

4

Name: _____

The Colors of Me

Directions

1. **Write** your name on the line above.
2. **Read** each sentence.
3. **Color** the crayons next to each sentence.
4. **Color** the five crayons in the box to show all the colors you used.

My eyes are this color:

My hair is this color: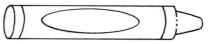

My favorite color is:

This is one of the colors I am wearing today:

If I could paint my classroom any color, I would paint it: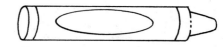

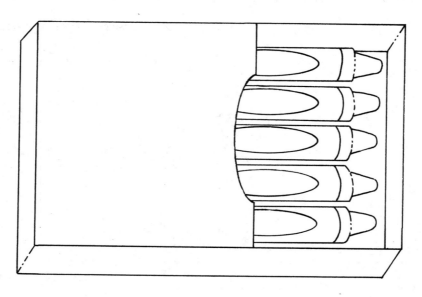

Follow-the-Directions: All About Me
© 2012 by Kama Einhorn,
Scholastic Teaching Resources

14

Name: _____

Meet My Friend

Directions

1. **Write** your name on the line above.

2. **Color** the picture to look like one of your friends.

3. **Write** your friend's name underneath.

4. **Circle** two things you like to do with your friend.

Read books.

Play games.

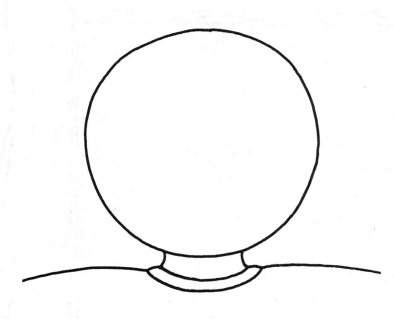

Do puzzles.

Share a snack.

_____
My Friend's Name

Go to the playground.

Name: _____

People in My Family

Directions

1. **Write** your name on the line above.

2. **Trace** the words "My Family" below.

3. In the frame, **draw** the people in your family.

4. **Write** their names below their pictures.

My Family

Follow-the-Directions: All About Me © 2012 by Kama Einhorn, Scholastic Teaching Resources

Name: _____

Meet Someone in My Family

This is my _____.

His/her name is _____.

Name: _____

Where I Live

Directions

1. **Write** your name on the line above.
2. **Circle** the number of people who live with you.
3. **Underline** the number of pets that live with you.
4. In the box, **draw** a picture of where you live and who lives with you.

0   1   2   3   4   5   6   7   8

9   10   11   12   13   14   15

Name: _____

Family Fun

Directions

1. **Write** your name on the line above.
2. **Circle** the thing you like to do most with your family.
3. **Underline** what you last did with your family.
4. In the box, **draw** yourself having fun with your family.

Play games.

Bake cookies.

Go to the park.

Eat meals.

Read together.

Watch TV.

Name: _____

My School

Directions

1. **Write** your name on the line above.

2. In the circle, **write** the number that tells how many kids are in your class.

3. In the rectangle, **write** your teacher's name.

4. In the big box, **draw** your favorite thing to do in school.

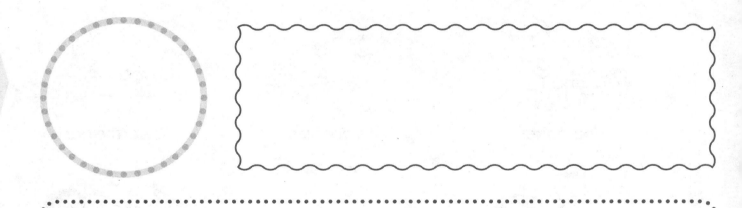

Name: _____

Things I Like to Do

1. **Write** your name on the line above.
2. **Circle** all the things you like to do.
3. **Underline** the thing you like to do most.
4. **Draw** yourself doing something else you like to do.
   Fill in the blank to complete the sentence.

Read books.

Write stories.

Play sports.

Paint pictures.

Sing songs.

I also like to

_____.

Play games.

Use the computer.

Follow-the-Directions: All About Me © 2012 by Kama Einhorn, Scholastic Teaching Resources

Name: _____

Playground Fun

Directions

1. **Write** your name on the line above.

2. **Look** at the pictures at the bottom of the page.
   Choose three of your favorite things to do on the playground.

3. **Color** them, then **cut** them out.

4. **Glue** them onto the playground.

 Jump rope.

 Play ball.

 Run.

 Swing.

 Climb.

 Slide.

Name: _____

My Quilt Design

Directions

1. **Write** your name on the line above.

2. **Draw** a picture in the middle square.

3. **Decide** what colors the other 4 squares will be. **Color** them.

4. **Decide** what colors the 16 triangles will be. **Color** them.

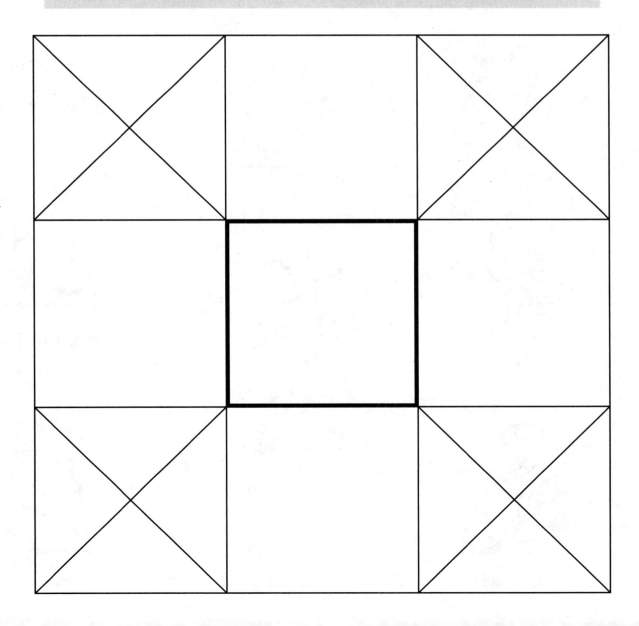

Name: _____

My Body Can...

Directions

1. **Write** your name on the line above.
2. **Circle** the things you like to do with your body.
3. **Put** an **X** on one thing you do not like to do.
4. **Underline** something you would like to learn to do.

Ice skate.

Jump.

Swim.

Run.

Skateboard.

Do gymnastics.

Ride a bike.

Climb.

Dance.

Name: _____

It's Time!

Directions

1. **Write** your name on the line above.

2. **Trace** the numbers on the clock.

3. **Look** at a clock. What time is it? **Show** the time on the clock below. **Draw** a long hand and a short hand.

4. **Circle** the times you wake up and go to bed.

 What time do you wake up on a school day?

- before 6:30 a.m.

- between 6:30 and 7:30 a.m.

- after 7:30 a.m.

 What time do you go to bed on a school night?

- before 8:30 p.m.

- 8:30 p.m.

- after 8:30 p.m.

My Birthday

Directions

1. **Write** your name on the line above.

2. How old will you be on your next birthday?
   Draw that number of candles on the cake.

3. **Fill in** the blanks below the cake.

4. **Color** the cake as you **sing** or **hum** the Happy Birthday song.

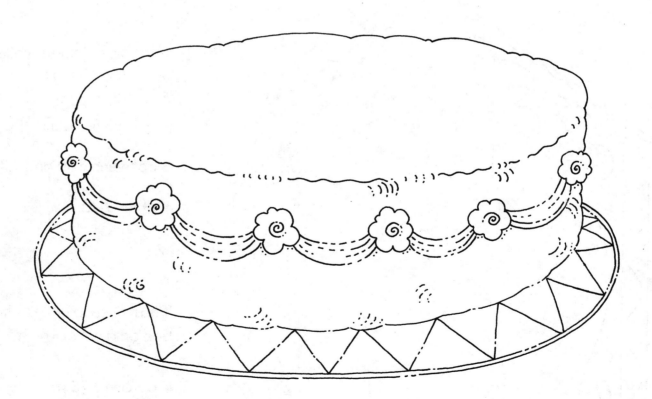

My birthday is on _____.

I will be _____ years old.

Name: _____

Here Comes Halloween!

Directions

1. **Write** your name on the line above.

2. **Circle** the Halloween treat you like best.

3. **Put** an **X** on the costume you think is most funny.

4. **Draw** two △ eyes and a ○ nose on the pumpkin. **Add** a mouth.

Treats

candy   raisins   stickers
corn

Costumes

alien   clown   monster

Extra! **Draw** yourself in the costume you would wear!

Name: _____

Thanks at Thanksgiving

Directions

1. **Write** your name on the line above.
2. **Color** all the things you are thankful for.
3. **Circle** the thing you are most thankful for.
4. In the box, **draw** something else you are thankful for.

my family

love

my teacher

pets

friends

food

toys

Name: _____

Happy New Year!

Directions

1. **Write** your name on the line above.

2. **Color** the letters H, P, E, and R green.
   Color the letters A, Y, N, and W blue.

3. **Trace** the dotted numbers.

4. **Count down** from 10 to 1 and say, "Happy New Year!"

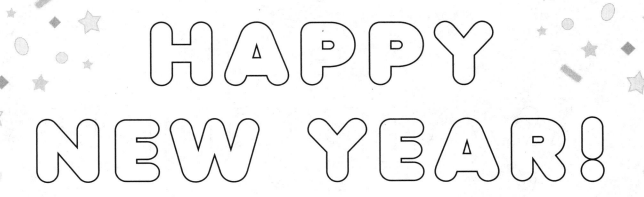

10   9   8   7   6   5   4   3   2   1

Extra!

Last year I stayed up until midnight on New Year's Eve.

Circle one: yes   no

Be My Valentine

Directions

1. **Write** your name on the line above.

2. **Look** at the pictures at the bottom of the page. **Circle** the gift you would give to your valentine.

3. **Color** the word "Valentine" in the heart red.

4. **Write** the name of your valentine on the line.

stuffed animal

Valentine card

box of candy

cupcake

flowers

My Favorite Season

Directions

1. **Write** your name on the line above.
2. **Underline** the name of your favorite season.
3. **Circle** the clothes you wear in that season.
4. In the box, **draw** something you like to do in your favorite season.

 winter  spring 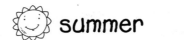 summer   fall

coat

flip-flops

pants

shorts

sweater

shirt

boots

T-shirt

sneakers

hat

Follow-the-Directions: All About Me © 2012 by Kama Einhorn, Scholastic Teaching Resources

Name: _____

My Favorite Breakfast

Directions

1. **Write** your name on the line above.
2. **Look** at the breakfast menu.
   Circle what you like to drink.
3. **Underline** two things you like to eat.
4. **Draw** a sun under the words "Good Morning."

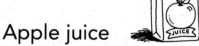 MENU

To Drink

Apple juice

Orange juice

Milk

To Eat

Cereal

Eggs

Pancakes

Yogurt with fruit

Good Morning!

Follow-the-Directions: All About Me
© 2012 by Kama Einhorn, Scholastic Teaching Resources

What's for Dinner?

Directions

1. **Write** your name on the line above.

2. **Look** at the foods below. **Cut** out the foods you want for dinner. **Glue** them to the plate.

3. What do you need to eat these foods—a fork? a spoon? a knife? **Color** the silverware you need.

4. **Write** the name of your favorite food on the line.

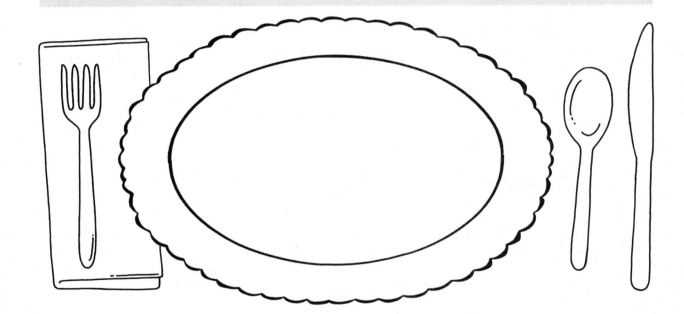

My favorite food is _____.

Follow-the-Directions: All About Me © 2012 by Kama Einhorn, Scholastic Teaching Resources

salad	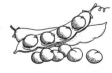 hamburger	peas	macaroni and cheese	soup
tacos	spaghetti and meatballs	carrots	rice	 chicken

My Favorite Pizza

Directions

1. **Write** your name on the line above.

2. **Check** the box below that tells how "cheesy" you like your pizza.

3. **Look** at the picture key. **Draw** foods you like on your pizza.

4. **Trace** the word "pizza" in red, below.

☐ My favorite pizza would have lots of cheese.

☐ My favorite pizza would have some cheese.

☐ My favorite pizza would have no cheese.

Picture Key

 broccoli

 pepperoni

 mushrooms

 peppers

 onions

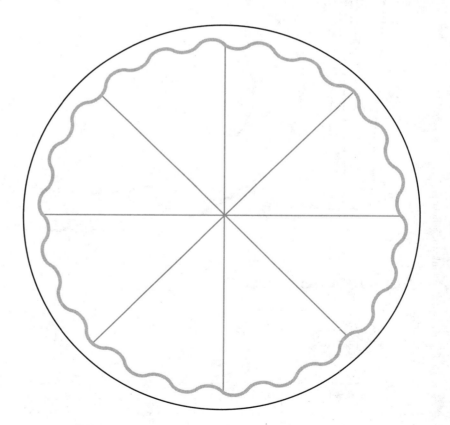

I made this pizza.

Name: _____

My Ice Cream Cone

Directions

1. **Write** your name on the line above.
2. **Color** the ice cream to look like your favorite flavor.
3. **Circle** the topping you want.
4. **Draw** the topping on your cone.

Toppings

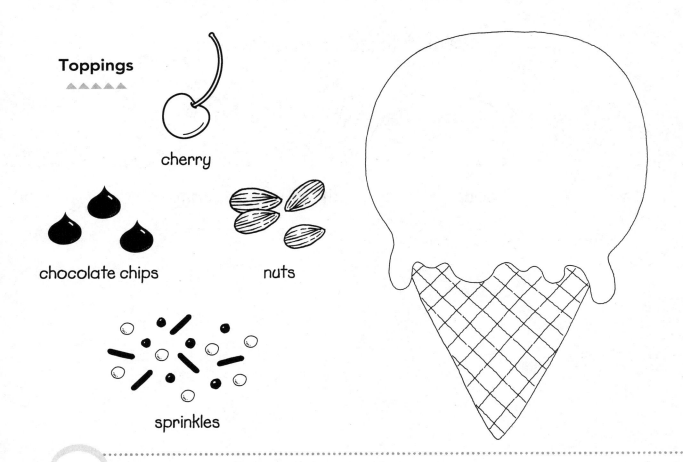

cherry

chocolate chips

nuts

sprinkles

Extra!   **Write** the name of your ice cream flavor here.

_____

Name: _____

Tasty Tastes

Directions

1. **Write** your name on the line above.
2. **Circle** your answer to the question below.
3. **Put** an **X** on the taste you like the least.
4. In the box, **draw** two favorite foods that have the taste you circled.

What taste do you like best?

      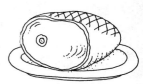

sweet   sour   bitter   salty   savory

Name: _____

Fruits and Vegetables

1. **Write** your name on the line above.

2. **Put** an **X** next to the fruits and vegetables you have tried.

3. **Underline** your two favorites.

4. **Circle** any fruit or vegetable you would like to try.

Fruits

Apple

Pear

Orange

Banana

Blueberries

Strawberries

Grapes

Peach

Pineapple

Cherries

Vegetables

Broccoli

Corn

Carrots

Peas

Asparagus

Beets

Green beans

Cauliflower

Sweet potato

Zucchini

Name: _____

My Pet

Directions

1. **Write** your name on the line above.

2. **Think** about a pet—real or pretend.
   What kind of animal is it? **Circle** your answer.
   Or, **add** your own idea on the line below the pictures.

3. **Draw** your pet in the box.

4. **Write** your pet's name above the picture.

My pet is a:

My pet's name:

cat

dog

bird

_____

fish

snake

turtle

iguana

rabbit

mouse

Another kind
of pet: _____

Name: _____

At the Zoo

Directions

1. **Write** your name on the line above.
2. **Circle** the big animal you would most like to see at the zoo.
3. **Underline** the reptile you would most like to see.
4. **Put** an **X** on the bird you would most like to see.

Big Animals

hippo

giraffe

elephant

polar bear

Reptiles

snake

alligator

lizard

turtle

Birds

flamingo

owl

penguin

parrot

Extra! **Color** all the animals.

Follow-the-Directions: All About Me
© 2012 by Kama Einhorn, Scholastic Teaching Resources

Name: _____

If I Could Be an Animal

Directions

1. **Write** your name on the line above.

2. **Look** at the animal pictures.
   Which animal would you be?

3. **Circle** that animal and **color** it.

4. **Underline** where you would live.

fish

cat

bird

monkey

I would live in

a house

a rainforest

the sea

a nest

Extra!

Write one thing you would like to do as that animal.

I would _____

_____

Follow-the-Directions: All About Me © 2012 by Kama Einhorn, Scholastic Teaching Resources

Name: _____

My Imaginary Creature

Directions

1. **Write** your name on the line above.
2. **Check** the boxes that tell about your creature.
3. **Fill in** the blanks with numbers.
4. **Draw** your creature in the box.

☐ My creature has fur.

☐ My creature has feathers.

☐ My creature has fur <u>and</u> feathers.

☐ My creature does not have fur <u>or</u> feathers.

My creature has _____ eyes.

My creature has _____ arms.

My creature has _____ legs.

If I Were a Cat

Directions

1. **Write** your name on the line above.

2. **Pretend** you are a cat.
   Circle the three things you would most like to do.

3. **Trace** the letters that spell "CAT."

4. **Color** the cat the way you would like to look.

Eat.

Sleep.

Scratch.

Hide.

Snuggle.

Play.

Climb.

Jump.

C A T

Follow-the-Directions: All About Me © 2012 by Kama Einhorn, Scholastic Teaching Resources

Name: _____

My Perfect Day

Directions

1. **Write** your name on the line above.

2. **Look** at the pictures at the bottom of the page. What would you do on your perfect day?

3. **Color** four pictures. You can **draw** your own idea, too.

4. **Cut** out and **glue** the pictures in order below.

First, I would...	Then, I would...	Next, I would...	Last, I would...

Visit a zoo.

Go to the playground.

Play sports.

Build with blocks.

Build a snowman.

Swim.

Play with a friend.

My Dream Room

Directions

1. **Write** your name on the line above.

2. **Think** about what kind of bedroom you would like.

3. **Color** the walls how you would paint them.

4. **Look** at the things below. **Cut** out and **glue** the ones you would want in your room.

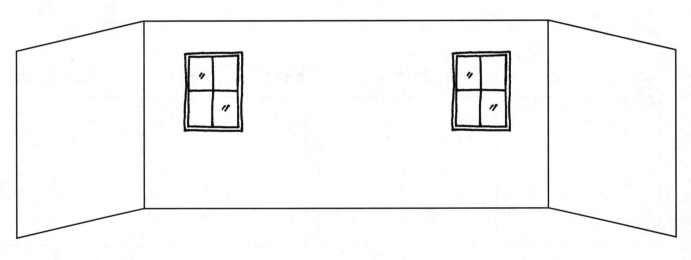

crazy clock · slide · cloud bed · tepee

zany robot · castle · merry-go-round · waterfall

Extra!

Draw other things in your room!

Name: _____

Building My Own Home

Directions

1. **Write** your name on the line above.

2. **Cut** out the windows and doors at the bottom of the page.

3. **Choose** the ones you want for your home. **Glue** them on.

4. **Draw** a roof on your home.

Name: _____

When I Grow Up

Directions

1. **Write** your name on the line above.

2. **Think** about a job you would like when you grow up.

3. **Check** the kind of job you might want.

4. In the box, **draw** yourself as a grown-up doing your job.

I would like to have a job:

☐ making or selling things. ☐ helping people or animals. ☐ entertaining people.

Name: _____

If I Could Go Anywhere

Directions

1. **Write** your name on the line above.
2. **Circle** the place you would most like to visit.
3. **Write** the place name on the postcard.
4. **Draw** a picture of that place on the postcard.

rainforest

desert

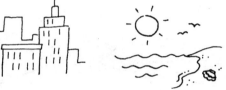
city

beach

mountains

Hello from the _____!

Name: _____

If I Could Fly

Directions

1. **Write** your name on the line above.
2. **Color** the flying or floating thing you would most like to be.
3. **Check** the sentences that are true.
4. In the box, **draw** what you would like to see from far above.

      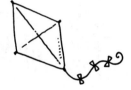      

bird   airplane   kite   rocket   hot air balloon

☐ It would be fun to fly.   ☐ It would be scary to fly.   ☐ It would be both fun and scary to fly.